Young Naturalist
Field Guides

Caterpillars, Bugs, and Butterflies

by Mel Boring

illustrations by Linda Garrow

Gareth Stevens Publishing
MILWAUKEE

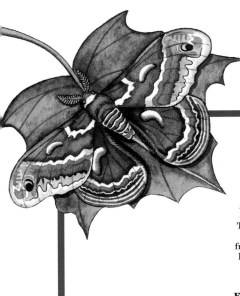

DEDICATION

For Zack, my son and research assistant, with love

ACKNOWLEDGMENTS

A book is never made by one person, and I want to thank two special people among the many who helped make this one. Thank you, Dr. Orley R. "Chip" Taylor of the University of Kansas Entomology Department and his Monarch Watch program for helping me get to know caterpillars and butterflies like friends. Thank you, Dr. Barbara Stay of the University of Iowa Department of Biological Sciences for showing me how bugs and caterpillars and butterflies are all close cousins.

For a free color catalog describing Gareth Stevens' list of high-quality books and multimedia programs, call 1-800-542-2595 (USA) or 1-800-461-9120 (Canada). Gareth Stevens Publishing's Fax: (414) 225-0377. See our catalog, too, on the World Wide Web: http://gsinc.com

Library of Congress Cataloging-in-Publication Data

Boring, Mel, 1939-
    Caterpillars, bugs, and butterflies / by Mel Boring; illustrated by Linda Garrow.
      p. cm. — (Young naturalist field guides)
    Originally published: Minocqua, Wis.: NorthWord Press, © 1996, in series: Take-along guide. With new index.
    Includes bibliographical references and index.
    Summary: An introduction to the world of caterpillars, butterflies, and other insects, including identification information, educational activities, and fun facts.
    ISBN 0-8368-2040-1 (lib. bdg.)
    1. Insects—Juvenile literature. 2. Caterpillars—Juvenile literature. 3. Butterflies—Juvenile literature. [1. Caterpillars. 2. Butterflies. 3. Insects] I. Garrow, Linda, ill. II. Title. III. Series.
QL467.2.B68 1998
595.7—dc21   97-31858

This North American edition first published in 1998 by
Gareth Stevens Publishing
1555 North RiverCenter Drive, Suite 201
Milwaukee, Wisconsin 53212 USA

Based on the book, *Caterpillars, Bugs and Butterflies*, written by Mel Boring, first published in the United States in 1996 by NorthWord Press, Inc., Minocqua, Wisconsin. © 1996 by Mel Boring. Illustrations by Linda Garrow. Book design by Lisa Moore. Additional end matter © 1998 by Gareth Stevens, Inc.

Printed in Mexico

1 2 3 4 5 6 7 8 9 02 01 00 99 98

CONTENTS

Caterpillars, Bugs and Butterflies

Metric Conversion Table
mm = millimeter = 0.0394 inch
cm = centimeter = 0.394 inch
m = meter = 3.281 feet

Note: Metric equivalents below are rounded off.

0.25 inch = 0.63 cm (6.3 mm)	5 feet = 1.5 m
1 inch = 2.5 cm (25 mm)	10 feet = 3 m
10 inches = 25 cm	15 feet = 4.6 m
12 inches (1 foot) = 30 cm	25 feet = 7.6 m
1 foot = 0.3 m	100 feet = 30 m
3 feet = 0.9 m	300 feet = 91 m

INTRODUCTION

Caterpillars and bugs and butterflies are all members of one big "family"—the insects. Most of the time, we just call them all bugs. But how could they all be from the same family? They don't look alike at all. The little black ant looks as different from the huge cecropia moth as a mouse from an elephant.

All caterpillars, bugs, and butterflies have one thing in common: change. The changing they do is easiest to see when a caterpillar becomes a butterfly. That is a complete change, from one creature to another. It makes them totally different creatures. This change is called metamorphosis.

A bug like the grasshopper is changing all the time, too. A grasshopper nymph "child" has a short body and legs that look too big for it. As it grows, its body slowly becomes longer and sleeker. And it grows wings for flying. These changes happen little by little.

This *Young Naturalist Field Guide* will help you learn about the many stages of insect life — nymph, grub, pupa, larva, cocoon, chrysalis, and more. You can use the ruler on the back cover to measure what you find. Bring a notebook and a pencil to draw what you see.

Have fun exploring the amazing world of caterpillars, bugs, and butterflies.

CATERPILLARS

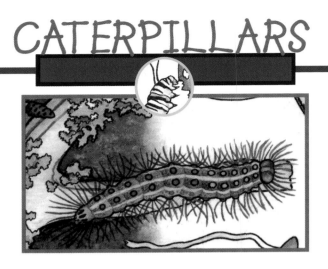

The caterpillar that crawls out of its egg is called a larva. It can only crawl about three feet a minute, so it hides from enemies on the bottoms of leaves. That's where you will find most caterpillars. A larva eats nonstop for about a month. It outgrows its skin and bursts through it several times as it grows. When a larva pops out of its last skin, it becomes a pupa.

The pupa stage is a short "rest stop" before it becomes an adult. Pupas don't eat, they just rest. Maybe they're saving up energy to fly.

The complete change from larva to adult happens while it is a pupa. When a butterfly caterpillar sheds its last skin, its inner skin hardens into a chrysalis. A moth caterpillar doesn't make a chrysalis. It makes a cocoon. First, it hooks a silk strand to the top of a twig. Next, it fastens that same thread to the bottom of the twig. Then it hangs head-down and spins threads across for the rest of the cocoon.

Find a chrysalis or cocoon and watch the new butterfly or moth emerge!

CABBAGE BUTTERFLY CATERPILLAR

What It Looks Like

The cabbage caterpillar is green or tan. Its skinny body grows no longer than your thumb. It looks like a tiny cucumber, so it can easily hide on a plant, and is hard to find. It is the first bug of spring and can be found in any garden cabbage patch.

What It Eats

The cabbage caterpillar was named for its favorite food. It also eats broccoli, cauliflower and radishes. And it likes mustard plants and some flowers. It is covered with velvety fuzz.

The yellow-billed cuckoo is one of few birds that eat this caterpillar. Other birds don't like to eat such a fuzzy meal.

On quiet days, if there are many cabbage caterpillars attacking a cabbage patch, you can actually hear them chewing!

Where to Find It

Look closely to find this caterpillar because it will be hiding its skinny body behind a fat leaf or a thin stem. In the woods, you will find cabbage caterpillars where trees are not too close together. They also like the open space of a farm field. And of course, look in cabbage patches.

MONARCH BUTTERFLY CATERPILLAR

What It Looks Like

Here's a caterpillar that looks like a little candy stick. Its white, yellow and black rings might look like peppermint, lemon and licorice to you. But to birds and other enemies, they are colors of DANGER, telling sparrows, chickadees and blue jays to keep away.

This caterpillar is about the size of your middle finger, and it can squeeze shorter or longer like an accordion.

What It Eats

The monarch caterpillar eats mostly milkweed. That bitter-tasting weed makes it taste terrible, because milkweed contains natural poisons. They don't harm the caterpillar, but they make its enemies sick. So hardly anything eats this caterpillar.

Where to Find It

You can see the monarch butterfly caterpillar from April through September. It lives in open areas like meadows and fields, and on roadsides—wherever milkweeds grow.

Its egg is smaller than a pinhead. Yet, in the first two weeks of its life, the monarch caterpillar grows to 2,700 times its birth-size. An 8-pound human baby growing at the same rate would weigh over 10 TONS at two weeks old!

TIGER SWALLOWTAIL CATERPILLAR

What It Looks Like

This plump green caterpillar has two large black and yellow "eyes" staring out of its bulging head. They are not eyes that see, but "eyespots." Its real eyes are smaller. They are on its head, too, in front of and below the eyespots.

If its scary-looking eyespots don't frighten birds away, the tiger swallowtail raises its red "stink gun." It is a Y-shaped "horn" found behind its head. It oozes bad-smelling goo to drive enemies away.

What It Eats

You can look for the tiger swallowtail caterpillar on a wide variety of trees and shrubs. It eats leaves from mid May to mid July.

Where to Find It

This caterpillar rests on a pad of its own silk all day, with a leaf curled around it like a blanket. It comes out at night to eat. It grows about as long as your middle finger.

Over winter, this caterpillar can be found as a pupa among the litter on the ground or on one of the trees it feeds on. It will look like an orange-brown piece of bark, with a silk thread holding it around the middle.

9

MOURNING CLOAK CATERPILLAR

What It Looks Like

The mourning cloak caterpillar is black with white speckles and a row of red diamonds on its back with black bristles. It has shiny eyes. It grows about as long as your ring finger.

When this caterpillar becomes a butterfly, its wings are mostly dark-colored, like old-fashioned funeral shawls worn by women. That is how they got the name "mourning cloak."

What It Eats

The mourning cloak caterpillar eats the leaves of elm, willow, cottonwood, poplar, birch, aspen or hackberry trees. Look for trees with leaves that have been eaten down to the "skeletons."

Where to Find It

Mourning cloak caterpillars can be found in open woodlands, and along riverbanks and forest edges. They gang up in groups big enough to strip all the leaves off young trees. They are easy to find in June and July.

Young mourning cloak caterpillars hang out together in webs. If you disturb their web, they wiggle like dancers dancing.

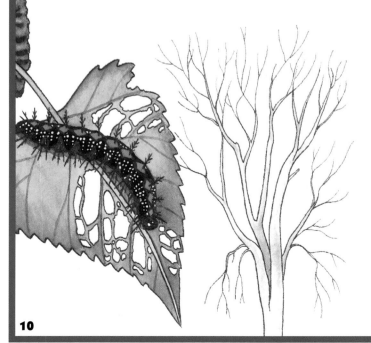

GYPSY MOTH CATERPILLAR

What It Looks Like

Gypsy moth caterpillars look like tiny parade floats. They are decorated with twelve bright red dots and ten blue dots down their backs. There are tufts of brown bristles along the sides of their bodies. The gypsy caterpillar grows about as long as your index finger.

What It Eats

These caterpillars always seem to be hungry. They eat the leaves of 400 kinds of trees—even pine tree needles. Every seven to ten years, from May to mid July, there is an outbreak of gypsy caterpillars in the Northeast, where most of them live. In their last big outbreak, they gobbled the leaves off 13 million acres of trees and shrubs.

Where to Find It

Look for gypsy moth caterpillars on the ground during the day. They eat in trees all night, but by day, they drop down into litter around the tree.

In its 8-week lifetime during the first half of summer, one caterpillar can eat a whole square yard of leaves. Assassin bugs eat gypsy moth caterpillars.

BANDED WOOLLYBEAR

What It Looks Like

The banded woolly-bear caterpillar is easiest to find in autumn. By then it has a wide brown stripe around its middle and black on both ends. This thumb-sized caterpillar rolls up into a ball when disturbed.

Some people say the woollybear can forecast the weather. The more black it has, legend says, the colder the winter will be. But scientists say it grows less black as it gets older. So a woollybear with more black is really just a younger caterpillar.

What It Eats

The woollybear eats garden plants and clover in the summer. Its enemies are mostly birds. But most birds don't like such fuzzy food, so they don't eat too many.

Where to Find It

In fall you will see it crawling out of gardens, over lawns, even across highways. In spring, the woollybear caterpillar spins its cocoon out of its body hair and silk. It becomes the isabella moth, a member of the tiger moth family. So, the "bear" turns into a "tiger."

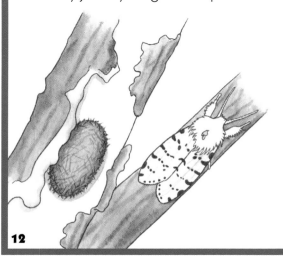

CECROPIA MOTH CATERPILLAR

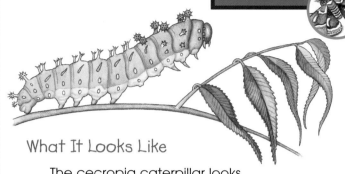

What It Looks Like

The cecropia caterpillar looks kind of scary. It has a row of dinosaur-like spikes down its back. The front ones look like clubs with knobs on the ends. Cecropia caterpillars are apple-green.

What It Eats

This giant caterpillar uses its huge mouth parts to find food, since it is nearly blind. It has strong senses of touch and taste.

Where to Find It

Cecropia eggs are laid in the spring on elm, willow, ash or lilac trees. But as this caterpillar grows, it may move to a greater variety of trees and shrubs.

Look for its tough, brown or gray, big-bag cocoon firmly attached to a twig. The cocoon is easily found in winter when trees are bare. Sometimes you might find the cecropia making its pupa in the ground, instead of in a cocoon on a tree. Cecropia caterpillars become cecropia moths in the spring.

TOMATO HORNWORM

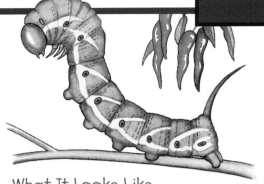

What It Looks Like

The tomato hornworm's rear "horn" looks frightening. This caterpillar rears its head back as if it wants to fight when you touch it. People think it stings or is poisonous, but it is not. In fact, its scary "horn" is soft, and not harmful at all.

The tomato hornworm is green, with a row of yellow arrowheads along each side pointing toward its head.

What It Eats

Tomato hornworms gobble up the leaves of tomato plants, and sometimes the tomato itself. Tomato hornworms also eat the leaves of peppers, eggplants and weeds. You will see them in summer in the garden.

Where to Find It

Birds are the main enemies of this caterpillar. But it makes a tiny squeak to frighten them away. It also hides on plants. The arrowheads on its sides look like leaf veins, so it probably doesn't look very tasty to enemies.

When it is a month old, and longer than the width of your hand, the tomato hornworm lowers itself to the soil on a silk thread and buries itself underground. Out comes the sphinx moth in spring.

CAPTURE A "BEAR" FOR THE WINTER

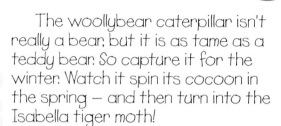

The woollybear caterpillar isn't really a bear, but it is as tame as a teddy bear. So capture it for the winter. Watch it spin its cocoon in the spring — and then turn into the Isabella tiger moth!

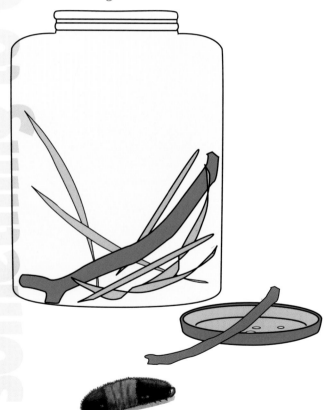

WHAT TO DO

1 Find a brown and black banded woollybear caterpillar in October, crawling across the lawn or garden.

2 Put it in a clear plastic collecting jar with holes in the lid.

3 Put a twig or two in the jar and some fresh green grass for it to eat. Put fresh grass in every day. It will perch on the twig for a few days or a week. Then it will lie down to sleep on the bottom.

4 Carefully take out any remaining grass, but leave the twigs in the jar all winter long.

5 Keep it in a place outside that is protected from bad weather. You will be able to watch it hibernate.

6 In spring, when weeds start to turn green outside, the woollybear will need food. Feed it fresh grass every day. Then watch it spin its "magic" cocoon of silk and hair.

7 In a week or so, it will become the Isabella tiger moth. On a nice day, take the moth outside and set the "tiger" free.

BUGS

The baby bug that hops out of its egg is called a nymph. Nymphs look a lot like the adults they will become in two or three months. Nymphs are fast hoppers—from plant to ground and back, unlike most caterpillars that stay put on their plants.

Nymphs eat a lot! Some eat as much as 16 times their weight each day. That would be like you eating 930 pounds of food every day. Nymphs outgrow and shed their skin many times before they become adults.

All true bugs have an "X" on their back. The crossing of their wings or wing covers make the "X." One wing overlaps the other when the bug is resting. You can see that the milkweed bug is a true bug by its red "X." But the June bug has no "X." It is born a larva, called a grub. It spends its life underground until it becomes an adult.

See how many true bugs you can find!

LITTLE BLACK ANT

What It Looks Like

There are 10,000,000,000,000,000—that's ten million billion—ants in the world! In fact, there are more ants than all the rest of the insects put together. One little black ant is only half as big as a grain of rice.

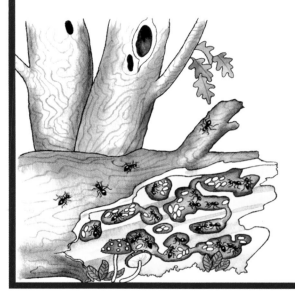

What It Eats

Ants eat other insects and fruit, and whatever crumbs they can find. Frogs, birds, spiders and other insects eat ants.

Ants "talk" to each other using scent signals. When a little black ant finds a crumb, it hauls it back to the nest. And it leaves a scent trail from its bottom. Other ants will follow the trail to find more crumbs. If you rub your finger across the scent trail ants make, the ant parade will stop. You rubbed away the smell that led them to the food.

Where to Find It

Little black ants live everywhere, but usually near trees. Most ants are female. No ant lives alone, and all ants share their work. In winter, they move down to the deepest levels of the anthill. But in cold winter places, ants hibernate.

TRUE KATYDID

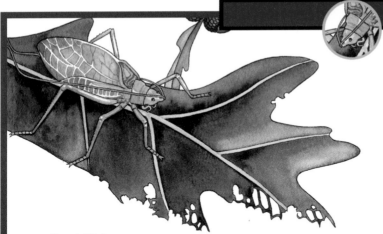

What It Looks Like

What insect says its own name? The katydid. It sounds like it is arguing with itself: "Katy did, Katy didn't, Katy did." It is hard to see Katydids, but if one is around you will surely hear it. Katydids grow about as long as your first finger. Each katydid has long antennae that run back and curl under its bottom.

What It Eats

Katydids are as green as the leaves they eat. Oak, maple, apple and cherry trees, and shrubs are their favorites. They hide from birds during the day by looking like leaves. At night bats eat them.

Where to Find It

Katydids lay eggs in the fall on the loose bark of trees, and on leaf stems. Katydid nymphs hatch in the spring without their wings. They grow them as they become adults.

The male katydid makes a special call at night. One of his wings is like a violin and the other is like a bow. He rubs one wing over the other, playing a love song that is heard by female katydids up to one mile away.

FIREFLY

What It Looks Like

This bug is also known by other names like lightning bug and glowworm. But it is really a beetle—with lights. When full-grown, the firefly is almost as long as the width of your thumb. Its wing covers are blackish-brown, with dull yellow borders. Female fireflies do not fly.

Even the larva of the firefly glows. The glow makes light but not heat. Oxygen mixes with body fluids in the firefly's tail and makes "cold light." The firefly turns its light on by sending oxygen to its tail, and stops the oxygen to turn it off.

What It Eats

Most fireflies eat nothing because their lives are so short. Those that do eat pollen, nectar and other soft-body insects.

Where to Find It

Fireflies use their lights to attract a mate. You can see them find each other on your lawn or in an open field, after sunset in June through August.

The firefly's enemies don't seem to be afraid of its light. In fact, sometime you may find a frog with a light glowing in its tummy. It is not an alien—it just swallowed a firefly!

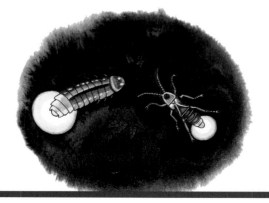

JUNE BUG

What It Looks Like

The June bug is the "tank" of the insect world. It is built like a stout box and can grow to be nearly as long as your nose.

When June bugs fly, they look like double-wing airplanes, with wingcases held high so their flight wings can move freely. Their legs and antennae are spread out like radar.

Where to Find It

Its name could be "May beetle" because it is really a beetle, and you often see it in late May. By June, you will hear it before you see it—buzzing against your open window screens. It is reddish-brown and oval-shaped. If you hold your magnifying glass over its antennae, they look like tiny moose antlers.

What It Eats

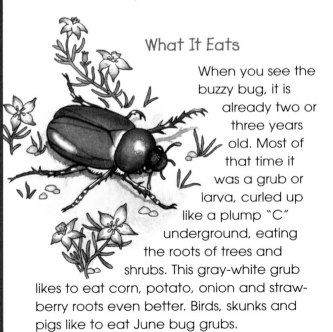

When you see the buzzy bug, it is already two or three years old. Most of that time it was a grub or larva, curled up like a plump "C" underground, eating the roots of trees and shrubs. This gray-white grub likes to eat corn, potato, onion and strawberry roots even better. Birds, skunks and pigs like to eat June bug grubs.

FIELD CRICKET

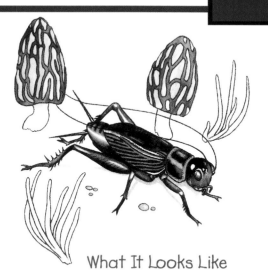

What It Looks Like

The field cricket is about the size of your eye. Its head is as wide as its body, and the antennae reach down past its bottom. Field crickets are black, with red-brown stripes on their wing covers. They have short wings.

Crickets have wings that "sing" by rubbing against each other. A cricket can be a "ventriloquist," lowering its "voice" when you are near, to make it sound far away. But look close around you, it may be right at your feet!

What It Eats

Crickets eat other insects, including each other, and dead animal remains. They also eat plants like tomatoes, peas, and beans. Mammals, reptiles, and spiders eat crickets. But their worst enemies are birds.

Where to Find It

Adult crickets appear by July and August. Look for the field cricket on your lawn, in fields and woods, as well as along roadsides—wherever you hear them chirping. Check under things for them, too, such as rocks and logs.

LATERAL LEAFHOPPER

What It Eats

Leafhoppers stab their dagger beaks into a plant's sap stream like vampires. As leafhoppers go from leaf to leaf, they leave behind a sweet-tasting liquid called "honeydew." Flies, bees and wasps like to eat it. They eat leafhoppers, too. So do sparrows.

What It Looks Like

Most leafhoppers are smaller than your little fingertip. A lateral leafhopper is black with brown stripes making a "V" between its wings. Its body is slender and oval. It has a stabbing "beak" used to sip plant juices. The beak is under the head.

"Lateral" means "sideways," and lateral leafhoppers have the unusual ability to run sideways. Leafhoppers are called "dodgers" too. When the plants they are on are disturbed, adult leafhoppers hop or fly away sideways and duck under the leaf. So always turn the leaves over very carefully.

Where to Find It

Lateral leafhoppers are easiest to find in June, July and August because by then they are full grown. You will find them on weeds and grasses, flowers (especially asters) and trees—nearly everywhere.

LADYBIRD BEETLE

What It Looks Like

You probably know this beetle by another name: Ladybug. It can fly. And of course, not all ladybugs are ladies—some are males. The ladybug is the world's favorite bug. In some parts of Germany, the ladybug, and not the stork, is said to bring newborn babies.

This shiny, round bug comes in different colors: red, orange, yellow, brown, tan or gray. It may have polka dots or stripes. Some have as many as 22 spots. And some have no spots at all. But most ladybugs have black spots on red or orange wing covers.

What It Eats

Aphids are a ladybug's favorite food. They also eat leafhoppers, mites and other small insects.

No bug eats ladybugs, because they squirt stinky goo from their knees. The goo is poisonous, but only to other bugs.

Where to Find It

You will find ladybird beetles in your garden, on flowers, grapes, apples, potatoes or corn.

MILKWEED BUG

What It Looks Like

The milkweed bug is named for the plants it eats. Milkweed bugs are oval-shaped, and no longer than the width of your finger. They lay eggs on milkweed plants when the leaves and flowers come out in spring.

The milkweed bug has warning colors to show its enemies it is poisonous to eat. Some bugs have warning colors, but are not poisonous. But bright orange monarch butterflies, red-orange ladybugs, and red milkweed bugs are poisonous to eat and flash like "stop lights" to their enemies.

What It Eats

They eat and live on milkweeds all summer until the first frost. Then they dive into leaf litter, logs, or into houses and hibernate over winter.

Where to Find It

This bug is sluggish and slow. It usually flies straight with no tricky twists, so it is not hard for birds and spiders to catch. That is why it does not fly unless it has to, but stays hidden under leaves. Look for it wherever there are a lot of milkweeds.

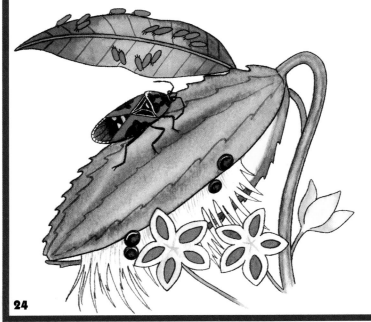

PERIODICAL CICADA

What It Looks Like

The periodical cicada is black or brown, about an inch long, with bulging, glowing red eyes and see-through wings. Look for it in July and August. It may look fierce, but it doesn't bite or sting.

Periodical cicadas spend either 13 or 17 years growing underground. Then the nymphs climb up the nearest tree or post and shed their skin. Adults live only 40 to 60 days. If your life cycle was like the periodical cicada's, you would spend 71 years growing up!

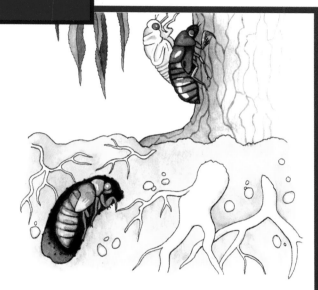

What It Eats

Cicada nymphs suck juice from plant roots. Adult cicadas feast on tender tree twigs and leaves.

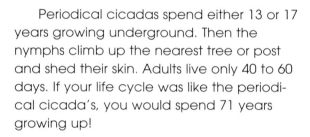

Where to Find It

The cicada's buzz sounds like a power saw cutting through metal. No other insect sounds like the cicada. The sounds come from the vibrations of the cicada's skin stretched over hollows on its body.

On summer evenings, you hear the cicada's "buzz saw." Find which trees the sounds came from, then look for the cicadas in daylight. Cicadas are hard to find, because they flatten themselves on the other side of a tree when they hear you coming—and then fly away fast.

NORTHERN WALKINGSTICK

What It Looks Like

Can sticks walk? Walkingstick insects can. But they only walk at night. In the daylight, they hold so still that they look exactly like little sticks with six legs. That is how they escape their bird enemies.

The northern walkingstick grows to be about as long as your first finger. Its relative, the giant walkingstick in the southern United States, grows to be almost six inches long. This walkingstick is one of the longest bugs in the world.

Sometimes, a walkingstick's leg may break off. But it can grow new ones. The new legs are never as big or strong as the originals, but there are still six.

What It Eats

Walkingsticks spend nearly their entire lives sitting still and chewing leaves around them. They eat locust, walnut, cherry and rose leaves. They especially like oak and hazelnut trees.

Where to Find It

Use a flashlight to find northern walking-sticks after dark. Look on the trees where they feed.

Since walkingsticks stay hidden by not moving, you might see one if you make it move. Shake a branch and watch the ground underneath it. You just might shake a "stick" off!

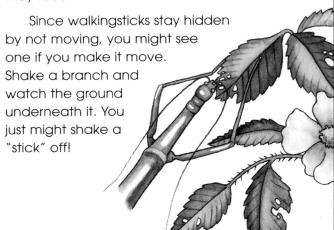

DRAGONFLY

What It Eats

Other insects are its only food—and it will even eat other dragonflies. Dragonflies carry a "food basket" with them. They curl their six legs inward, forming a "basket" to carry away the food they snatch while flying—dragonfly "fast food."

What It Looks Like

The "dragon" of all bugs is the dragonfly. And it is one quick bug. It flies up to 35 miles per hour.

The dragonfly has been around for over 300 million years. Today's green darner dragonfly fits on your hand. But prehistoric dragonfly wings spread almost 2 feet across!

To spot its food, the dragonfly has the most powerful eyes of any bug. Most of its head is covered with its enormous eyes. It can see you move when you are still about 20 steps away from it.

Where to Find It

The most common dragonfly is the green darner. It is about as long as your middle finger. You will find it wherever there is a pond nearby. Look for it in August or September on sunny days.

USE A "CRICKET THERMOMETER"

The warmer it is outside, the faster crickets chirp. You can figure out the temperature by counting cricket chirps and doing a little math.

70° F
- 40 chirps
_____
30 magic number

WHAT TO DO

1 To set up your "cricket thermometer" find out what the temperature is.

2 Listen to a cricket and count how many times it chirps in 15 seconds. Write that number down in a notebook.

3 Subtract that number from the temperature.

4 This is the "magic number." For example, if the temperature was 70°F (21°C), and your cricket chirped 40 times, your magic number would be 30.

Now you can figure out the temperature any time you want to. Just count the number of cricket chirps in 15 seconds and add your "magic number." The number you get is the temperature!

BUTTERFLIES AND MOTHS

When a butterfly or moth breaks out of its chrysalis or cocoon, it is wrinkled and wet. It pumps body fluids into its wings until they unfold and dry. Then it can fly.

Moths spend the rest of their short lives looking for places to lay their eggs. Most of them do not even take time to eat.

Butterflies fly in the daytime, but most moths fly at night. Butterflies' bodies are slender. Moths have chubby bodies. Butterfly antennae are thin and smooth, with small knobs at the end. Moths have thick, feathery antennae. Antennae are

their feelers and smellers. They use them to find food and mates.

An easy way to tell a butterfly from a moth is to watch it land: If its wings are folded together pointing up, it's probably a butterfly. If its wings are folded against its body or pointing out flat from its sides, it's probably a moth.

Butterflies and moths drink nectar with their proboscis—their tongue. It is long and curled up inside itself like a spring. They unroll this hollow tongue to sip the nectar—like you sip soda pop through a straw.

MONARCH BUTTERFLY

What It Looks Like

Monarch butterflies look "dressed up" for Halloween in bright orange and black. From May until November, the butterfly you see most is the monarch.

It is easy to tell which monarchs are male. They have mating scent sacs on their back wings. Each has a tiny bulge on the black line at the center of the wing. These attract female monarchs.

What It Eats

You will find monarchs mostly on milkweeds. But they also sip nectar from lilacs, red clover, thistle and goldenrod.

Most birds don't eat monarchs because the milkweed they eat makes them poisonous to birds. It doesn't hurt the monarch but it makes birds sick.

Where to Find It

Look for monarchs flying through your yard, stopping to sip from garden flowers.

Monarchs are famous for migrating (going to a warmer place for winter). Most monarchs fly to Mexico. Some fly 2,500 miles in six weeks. Scientists have learned that they fly as fast as 35 miles an hour. One flew 265 miles in one day. That's how they got their nickname "wanderers."

TIGER SWALLOWTAIL BUTTERFLY

What It Looks Like

It has stripes like a tiger and tails like a bird! Bright yellow and black tiger swallowtails are high fliers, so look for them above your head. From spring to September, they soar among the tall tree branches. They may zip out of sight, then pop back suddenly.

A tiger swallowtail's wings can stretch from one end of a dollar bill to the other—about 6 inches. Their wing tails can be as long as one inch.

What It Eats

Swallowtails sail about in flight for hours at a time. They flit above flowers, pausing only to sip nectar from lilacs, phlox or honeysuckle. Even while sipping they keep their wings beating.

Where to Find It

Usually, swallowtails stay in groups. You will sometimes see them sipping from the edges of a puddle or stream. Male swallowtails also need the sodium in the water so they will be able to mate.

Sometimes you can smell the sweet smells male swallowtails give off to lure female swallowtails.

RED ADMIRAL BUTTERFLY

The red admiral has been known to land on the shoulders of gardeners who were in their gardens day after day. If you spend lots of time where red admirals are, one of them may put its admiral's stripes on your shoulder.

What It Eats

Juice from rotting fruit and tree sap are food for red admirals. They also drink the nectar of thistle, milkweed, dandelion, red clover, daisies, asters and butterfly bushes.

What It Looks Like

The red admiral got its name from its orange wing stripes. They look like the stripes admirals in the navy wear on their uniforms. They fly very rapidly and ziggy-zaggy, so red admirals are hard to see up close. A red admiral's wide open wings are about the length of your middle finger.

Where to Find It

Red admirals sail into gardens and fields, along the edges of woods and rivers, and in barnyards. Afternoon or evening is the best time to see one on porch roofs, on shrubs or along sidewalks. At earlier, sunnier times, you will find them drinking from flowers or fruit.

CABBAGE BUTTERFLY

What It Eats

Cabbage butterflies like to eat what's in your garden, especially cabbages, radishes and nasturtium flowers.

The yellow on cabbage butterfly wings is poisonous to birds. That color comes from mustard plant flowers they sip nectar from.

Where to Find It

Some people don't appreciate the cabbage butterfly because it is found so often—especially anywhere there is cabbage and at almost anytime of the year except winter. It flies from the last frost of spring until the first frost of fall.

You can find cabbage butterflies in gardens, farm fields, open woodlands and cities. They are found around the flowers of mustard, milkweed, red clover, dandelion, dogbane, aster and lantana.

What It Looks Like

Cabbage butterfly wings are powdery-white on top and greenish-yellow on the bottom. The front wings have gray tips. Its wings spread only from about top to bottom of your little finger.

Cabbage butterflies have weak eyes. They may mistake a daisy for a mate if the flower is more than a foot away. They have a proboscis that is double-barreled.

Count the dots on a cabbage butterfly's wings: males have one, but females have two.

BUCKEYE BUTTERFLY

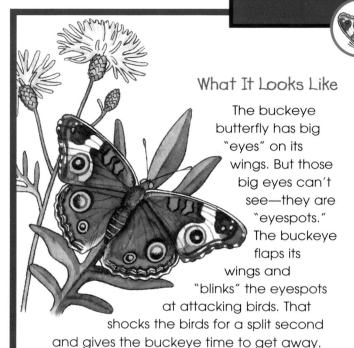

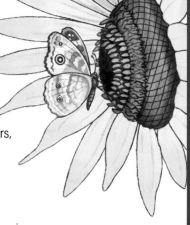

What It Looks Like

The buckeye butterfly has big "eyes" on its wings. But those big eyes can't see—they are "eyespots." The buckeye flaps its wings and "blinks" the eyespots at attacking birds. That shocks the birds for a split second and gives the buckeye time to get away.

Buckeyes are very colorful butterflies. They have bright red bars on their front wings. Those bars and their "eyes" and their scalloped wing shape help you recognize buckeyes easily. Buckeye wings spread about the length of your ring finger.

What It Eats

Sometimes the buckeye sips from mud puddles. It also sips nectar from asters, sunflowers, peppermint, knapweed and milkweed.

Where to Find It

You might find a buckeye sitting on the ground or beside the road on a sunny, hot day. It often pauses to bask in the sun with wings spread wide. You can find it in fields, meadows, or along roads from spring until fall.

Buckeyes play games of "air tag" with each other and other butterflies. They even chase grasshoppers that are over twice as long as they are!

PAINTED LADY BUTTERFLY

What It Looks Like

Most butterflies look as if they were carefully painted with a brush. But the painted lady butterfly looks like the paint box was dumped out on it. On top, it is rose, orange and brown, with black and white "paint spatters." Underneath, it is pink, gray, orange and brown, spattered with white and black and four bright eyespots.

Your ring finger will reach across the open wings of a painted lady.

What It Eats

Thistle flowers are the main places you will find the painted lady butterfly, sipping nectar. But also look for it on zinnia, cosmos, heliotrope, butterfly bush, mint, ironweed, red clover, milkweed and buttonbush.

Where to Find It

It flies wherever the land is open and bright, in gardens, parks, flowery meadows, deserts and mountains. Begin looking for this colorful butterfly in April until fall's first frost.

Painted ladies are found in more parts of the world than any other butterfly. So painted ladies have many names, like "Cynthia of the thistle" and "painted beauty."

GYPSY MOTH

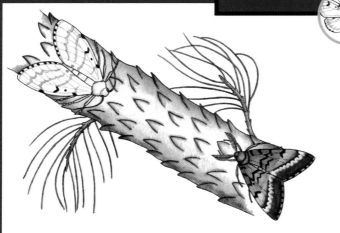

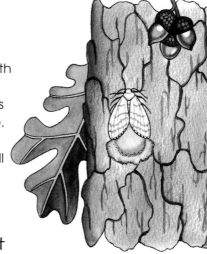

What It Eats

The gypsy moth does not eat anything during its one-week lifetime. It is as if it is living off energy from all the food it ate as a caterpillar.

What It Looks Like

One stormy night over a hundred years ago, the wind knocked over a cage of moths in Massachusetts. They had been brought from Europe. Some of them escaped. That is how the gypsy moth first got loose in the United States.

Gypsy moths have stout, hairy bodies. Males are brown with even darker brown markings. Females are white with brown marks. The male gypsy moth is smaller, too. Its body is less than an inch long. The female can spread her wings about 2 1/2 inches wide.

Where to Find It

You will find the gypsy moth in July and August, on pine and broadleaf trees, especially oak. They mate and lay their eggs on the trees.

Gypsy moths are day-fliers, unlike most moths. The male is a good flier, but the larger and heavier female just flutters along the ground. Gypsy moths have now spread as far south as West Virginia, and as far west as Minnesota and Texas.

CECROPIA MOTH

What It Eats

The cecropia moth does not eat. But you will find it on the same plants cecropia caterpillars eat: cherry, maple, willow, ash, and lilac. They rest at the base of trees, hidden on bark and dead leaves.

What It Looks Like

The cecropia may startle you with its color and size. Its wings are darker brown closer to the body and striped with gold, orange and yellow. All four wings have white and red half-moon shapes on them. A cecropia's open wings reach from your wrist to your fingertips.

The male cecropia moth is smaller, with a more feath-erlike body. In mating, female cecropias send out "love scents" to male cecropias as far away as two miles. Up close, cecropia moths smell like peanut butter!

Where to Find It

Watch for them during May and June evenings on window screens or around a porch light. Cecropias also fly by day, unlike most other moths. They like open country, with trees and bushes.

LUNA MOTH

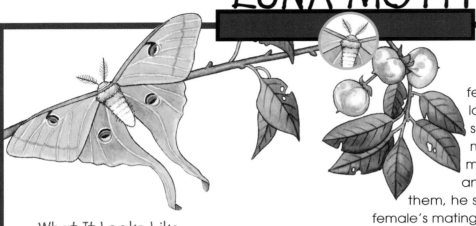

Male and female lunas look much the same. But the male has more feathery antennae. With them, he senses the female's mating perfume.

What It Looks Like

If you spot the spectacular luna moth, don't try to catch it. It is an endangered species.

The luna moth has very long tails. Its color is a glowing green, but it also has touches of purple, brown, yellow, white and gray. From wingtip to wingtip, it is a little shorter than your hand length. You may see it just beneath a streetlight, waggling its wings as if dancing. When its long, dangling tails sway in the breeze, it looks like a little lunar-green "moon kite."

What It Eats

Luna moths have no mouths or stomachs. They do not eat and only live about one week.

Where to Find It

As soon as the female comes out of the cocoon in April or June, she searches for a tree with leaves her offspring can eat. Many different trees could be food for her caterpillars. So you may find her on walnut, hickory, oak, birch, alder, sweet gum or persimmon trees.

MAKE "MOTH SUGAR"

Moths have antennae that look like miniature feathers. They work like radio aerials, picking up faraway signals. They can smell "moth sugar" from miles away. Wait until late afternoon to spread moth sugar so the sun will cook but not evaporate it.

WHAT YOU NEED

- 3 tablespoons sugar
- water
- 1 quart (1 liter) plastic jug
- old paintbrush
- sponge

WHAT TO DO

1 Fill the jug with water.

2 Mix sugar into the jug of water.

3 Use the paintbrush to brush the "moth sugar" on a stump, a rock, or a fence post. Or soak the sponge in the mixture and hang it on a tree.

4 Just after dark, go see your new visitors.

5 If no moths have come to the place, next time add a little apple juice to the "moth sugar."

There are more than 100,000 kinds of moths in the world. Many will be attracted to this tasty treat!

something to do

For More Information

MORE BOOKS TO READ

Ants: A Great Community. Secrets of the Animal World series. Andreu Llamas (Gareth Stevens)

Butterflies: Magical Metamorphosis. Secrets of the Animal World series. Eulalia García (Gareth Stevens)

Butterfly Magic for Kids. Animal Magic series. E. J. Norsgaard (Gareth Stevens)

Insects. Under the Microscope series. John Woodward (Gareth Stevens)

The New Creepy Crawly Collection series. (Gareth Stevens)

VIDEOS

The Bug Man of Ithaca. (New Dimension Media)

Insect Metamorphosis. (Phoenix/BFA Films and Video)

Insects and How They Live. (AIMS Media)

WEB SITES

www.tesser.com/minibeast/trivia.htm

//mgfx.com/butterfly/gallery/index.htm

INDEX